Sir Robert Borden

The shy guy who challenged an empire

Written by Irene Ternier Gordon

Illustrated by Bernie Mireault

Publisher— Jacqueline Brown
Editor — Greg Mazlak
Researchers — Barbara Baillargeon and Hagit Hadaya

JackFruit Press Ltd.
Toronto, Canada
www.jackfruitpress.com

Library and Archives Canada Cataloguing in Publication

Gordon, Irene Ternier
    Sir Robert Borden : the shy guy who challenged an empire / Irene Ternier Gordon ; Bernie Mireault, illustrator.

(Canadian prime ministers : warts & all)
Includes index.
ISBN 978-0-9736406-9-4

1. Borden, Robert Laird, Sir, 1854–1937—Juvenile literature.
2. Prime ministers—Canada—Biography—Juvenile literature.
3. Canada—Politics and government—1911-1921—Juvenile literature. I. Mireault, Bernie, 1965– II. Title. III. Series.

FC556.B67G67 2007   j971.061'2092   C2007-904590-1

Printed and bound in Canada

...So, I'm here to show you around this really cool series of books on great Canadians.

This book tells the story of Sir Robert Borden, Canada's eighth prime minister.

This shy, reluctant leader boldly led our country through World War I, then fought to gain us an international voice.

Contents

Hot topics

Sir Robert Borden: The man

Canada's eighth prime minister has a place of honour on our $100 bills. Although he was a shy man who did not enjoy speaking in public, he stood up for Canada and demanded that its voice be heard after its soldiers fought so valiantly in World War I. He ensured that Canada became an equal partner with Britain, rather than an obedient colony.

who led Canada in World War I

Sir Robert Laird Borden was a serious, hard-working, and intelligent man. He was also a rather shy man who reluctantly took on the leadership of the **Conservative party** and of Canada because he felt that it was his duty to accept the challenge. While he enjoyed the order and discipline of his work as a lawyer, he found that political life was chaotic, unruly, and undisciplined. He concluded that a life in politics was "absolutely unsuited to a man of my temperament, and the sooner I get out of it the better."

But Sir Robert did not leave politics. Instead, when called upon to replace **Sir Charles Tupper** as the head of the Conservative party in 1901, he took up the challenge. He did so despite the fact, as he wrote, "the Conservative party was at the nadir of its fortunes and **Sir Wilfrid Laurier** was then approaching the zenith of his power and influence."

Sir Wilfrid Laurier was the elegant star, leader of the **Liberal party** and prime minister of Canada in 1901. While Laurier was eloquent and became known as a brilliant orator and a great conciliator (good at getting two sides to agree upon a solution), people thought Sir Robert dull and not very good at making decisions. You could not find two different men! Many people didn't believe Sir Robert would make a good leader.

But Sir Robert eventually became Canada's leader because of his ability to concentrate on a task and not give up. He spent ten years as **Opposition** leader but was determined to return his party to the power it had once held under **Sir John A. Macdonald**.

Sir Robert finally became prime minister in 1911, just a few short years before Canada got embroiled in the Great War—the War to End All Wars—**World War I**. It was during this time that Canadian soldiers made their name by fighting valiantly and winning battles when the British and French could not. They fought in famous battles such as Vimy Ridge and **Passchendaele**, creating pride in the hearts of Canadians at home and abroad.

Like the soldiers, Sir Robert also fought. He fought against the arrogant British war generals and politicians, who did not want to allow Canada a voice in determining how the war should be fought. When Sir Robert declared that he would not send any more soldiers to the war front unless Canada's voice was heard, Great Britain listened. Then after the war, he ensured that Canada's voice was heard among all the great nations of the world.

Some historians say Sir Robert received the honour of being placed on the $100 bill for his leadership during such a difficult time. Others say his reputation as one of Canada's best leaders is undeserved because leaders can only "go with the flow" and achieve very little during global events like war.

This is the story of a poor farm boy who could not even build a haystack that stayed together, but who became the leader of a great nation. What made him drop his rake and rise to the challenge of helping to forge a great nation? Read on and discover this for yourself!

Want to know more? The words in bold are explained in the glossary at the back of the book.

Now that the war is over, Sir Robert insists that Canada be involved in the conference called to negotiate the terms of peace with Germany. But Britain's PM wants Canada to sit in on only some of the meetings.

Sir Robert is furious. Eventually, Britain gives in and agrees to let its dominions (Canada, New Zealand, and Australia) have a say. This move marks the beginning of a whole new relationship between Canada and Britain.

1857

Robert's first memory is a visit from the local minister. Three-year-old Robert was fascinated by the minister's bald head, so he climbed a chair to get a closer look. His mother gave him such a stern look for his rudeness that he never forgot it!

8

Chapter 1

Robert disturbs the local minister

1854
Robert is born on June 26.

1863
Robert goes to school at the Acacia Villa Academy.

1868
Robert becomes the assistant school master in classical studies.

He teaches in Horton, Nova Scotia.

1872
Robert travels to the United States and teaches in Matawan, New Jersey.

The Bordens' ancestors were among a group of immigrants from New England, USA, who moved to Nova Scotia to farm the land that the **Acadians** had been forced to leave in 1755.

Young Robert

Robert Laird Borden was born on June 26, 1854, on a farm at Grand Pré, Nova Scotia, along the Minas Basin at the eastern end of the Bay of Fundy. His parents were Andrew Borden and Eunice Laird. Andrew farmed and he was also the railway stationmaster in Grand Pré. He was an able man with excellent judgment. Unfortunately, he lacked energy and had limited ability in business. As a result, the Borden family was quite poor while Robert was growing up.

In contrast, Robert's mother Eunice possessed remarkable energy, high ambition, and unusual ability. She was a woman of strong character, who expected her children to work very hard. They had to do their share of farm work and get a good education.

9

Robert does not like chores. He could not stand hoeing vegetables, hated chopping wood for winter fires, and could not build a load of hay that would stay together.

Obviously, the farmer's life was not for him!

"Back to the lily!"

One of Robert's earliest memories was of a visit the local minister made to his home. Because all the men in his family had lots of hair, 3-year-old Robert was intrigued by the minister's shiny bald head. He pushed a chair over to where the minister sat and climbed onto it to get a closer look, but his mother thought he was being rude. His mother scolded him so sternly that Robert immediately jumped from the chair and never forgot his lesson in good behaviour—even writing about it years later in his autobiography.

Robert disliked farm work, but he admitted that the exercise "was beneficial and healthful." Robert, his brother John, and their friends enjoyed skating, playing hockey, and sledding during what little free time they had in winter. The boys used to pile high banks of snow on the steep hills near their home to make jumps. As they went over the jumps on their sleds, the sleds would fly high into the air before hitting the ground again. Once, Robert and his brother crashed. Their sled was smashed to pieces, but luckily they were not injured. The boys would yell out "Back the lily" to warn people below them on the hill to get out of the way.

Robert, John, and their friends could be described as very early snow-boarders, although the first real snowboard was not built until almost 100 years later.

Robert's early school days

Robert began attending a school called Acacia Villa Academy when he was nine, but he got much of his schooling by studying on his own in the evenings after working on the farm all day. Robert was organized. He would make timetables in which he would chart off the amount of time available; how much time could be spent on chores; and how much on each subject of homework. John often made fun of Robert because he was so serious and worked so hard. One day, John attached on his father's railway notices to Robert's timetable. The notice read, "All timetables of a previous date to be destroyed." Even his mother sometimes laughed at Robert's extreme seriousness.

Robert suddenly changed from a school boy to a working man shortly before he turned 15 years old. Robert greatly admired James Henry Hamilton, a young teacher at Acacia Villa Academy, who grew up on a farm near the Bordens'. One day, Mr. Hamilton had a disagreement with the principal over the pronunciation of a Greek word. As a result of the argument, Mr. Hamilton stormed out of the school, never to return. Robert was such a good student in Greek and other **classical studies** that the principal immediately offered him Mr Hamilton's job. Robert accepted it and he became a teacher three months before his 15th birthday. One day he was a student. The next day he found himself teaching his former classmates, many of whom were older than he was.

Like many other schools in his day, the curriculum in Robert's school comprised classical studies which included Greek and Latin. One day, one of the teachers has an argument with the principal and storms out of the school.

1868

Realizing that the teacher is not coming back, the principal offers the job to Robert because he is an excellent student in classical studies. One day he's a student; the next day he's teaching his former classmates, many of whom are older than he is since he is three months short of his 15th birthday.

Oooh— what a storm! According to reports of the day, many animals and about 100 people were killed throughout Atlantic Canada and the United States by the Saxby Gale.

Also, millions of dollars worth of property damage was done. Many kilometers of dikes and fences had to be rebuilt; much of the hay needed to feed thesurviving livestock over the winter was destroyed; fishermen lost their boats and wharves; and buildings were destroyed.

Robert taught for the next three years, although he found teaching rather difficult. Think of all the problems he would have encountered. He had to prepare and teach the lessons and mark assignments. He had to make the students behave and do their work in class. Knowing how young and how serious Robert was, do you think he would have had an easy time getting his students to behave? And even though Robert was now teaching, that did not mean he could neglect his chores on the farm. They still had to be done. Also, he had to study by himself in the evenings to complete his own education.

One of the worst storms

Robert never forgot one of the worst storms in Nova Scotia history, the Saxby Gale, which took place when he was 15. The storm was named after Lieutenant John Saxby of the British Royal Navy, who was an amateur astronomer. Ten months earlier, Saxby had written letters to several British newspapers predicting that the position of the moon in the night sky would result in a serious windstorm on October 5, 1869, although he did not know where it would hit. The Saxby Gale was actually a category-2 hurricane, with winds of up to 176 kilometres per hour, that began in the Caribbean in late September.

The Borden house was on a hill overlooking distant meadows along the Minas Basin. The average difference between high and low tides in the basin, which is famous for having the highest tides on earth, is 12 metres and it can be as much as 16 metres. As a result, the Acadians had diked the land to prevent it from flooding at high tide. When Robert went to bed on the night of October 4, he could see a broad sweep of 1,200 hectares of land from his window—an area the approximate size of 600 large city blocks. When he awoke the next morning, the meadows were completely covered by the ocean.

It took several days before the salt water slowly began to drain back into the sea. Even then, many areas were flooded again at high tide each day because it took weeks to repair all the dikes. The salt water damaged the land so severely it was difficult to grow anything on it for some time afterward.

Ten days after the gale ended, an area newspaper called the Amherst *Gazette* reported that the whole area was barren as far as the eye could see. Beautiful green fields had been turned into a muddy brown marsh that produced an unhealthy dismal fog and a sickening smell. Fences lay strewn in every direction, haystacks were ruined, and occasionally the carcass of a dead animal could be seen bleaching in the sun.

Although Robert is only 15 when the Saxby Gale hits Nova Scotia, he knows he will never forget it. With winds of 176 km/h, this hurricane is one of the worst storms in the history of the province.

The Borden house sits on a hill overlooking distant meadows along a basin famous for having the highest tides on earth. When Robert goes to bed on the night of October 4, he can see an area the size of about 600 city blocks. But when he wakes up the next morning, that whole area is completely covered by the ocean.

13

Returning to Nova Scotia after living in New Jersey for a year, Robert decides to become a lawyer by working as a law clerk in a Halifax law firm. It is a very difficult time for him.

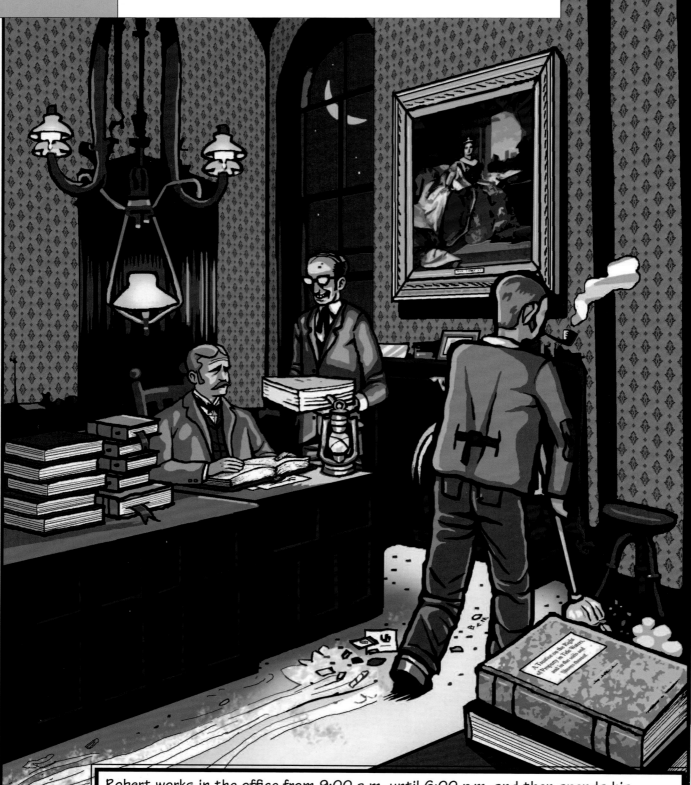

Robert works in the office from 9:00 a.m. until 6:00 p.m. and then spends his evenings studying. Everyone, including his family, thinks that he is working too hard and is too serious. One day, when Robert is looking particularly harassed, one of his colleagues says, "Cheer up, Borden; you'll have a nice long rest after you're dead."

Chapter 2

A legal career, marriage, and several pets

Robert wanted to go to university, but his family was too poor to send him. He could not even save the small salary he made by teaching because his parents needed this money to help support the family. Do you remember Mr. Hamilton, Robert's old teacher who stormed out of Acacia Villa Academy? Well, he had taken charge of a school in New Jersey after leaving Nova Scotia, and he offered Robert a position as a teacher in 1873. Robert accepted Mr. Hamilton's offer and left Grand Pré, Nova Scotia, for Matawan, New Jersey, in the United States. Robert only remained at Mr. Hamilton's school about a year before returning home. He feared that without completing university, he'd be doomed to teach in second-rate schools, surrounded by uninterested students. This future did not inspire him. An uncle convinced him to give law a try and he returned home to Nova Scotia.

At that time, many people did not go to university to study law. Instead they worked in law offices as articled clerks before being called to the bar. Robert spent four years as an articled clerk in a Halifax law firm. And, what a difficult time he had. Although the terms of Robert's articling job entitled him to apprentice in the practising of law, the senior

Laura and Robert loved dogs and cats. They had a St. Bernard named Taffy and a greyhound named Bobs.

Bobs really liked to sit in a certain armchair. Sometimes, when Robert was sitting on that chair, Bobs would put his head on Robert's knee and gaze at him, as if asking Robert to move.

Once, Laura was totally embarrassed when Bobs tried this trick on a visitor. When the lady leaned forward to pat Bobs on the head, he leaped in the air, as graceful as a ballet dancer, and landed between her back and the chair. That dog pushed the poor lady so hard that she almost fell on the floor!

lawyers in the firm were far too busy to give any attention whatever to Robert's legal education. Like other law students of the day, he worked in the office from 9:00 a.m. until 6:00 p.m., receiving next to no pay for keeping the account books. Once again, Robert worked during the day and studied in the evenings. This time, he was trying to master the mysteries of the law. Robert was so successful in mastering the mysteries of the law that he placed first of all the men who wrote the 1877 Nova Scotia **bar exams.**

Robert quickly became a successful lawyer. He practised law briefly in Halifax, facing the attorney general of Nova Scotia in his very first court case. Then he moved to Kentville where he gained experience in pleading cases before both the county and the **supreme courts.** He was so nervous when he had to defend clients in court that he could hardly eat or sleep for days. But since his nervousness did not show, few people knew how difficult he found court work.

In 1882, Robert was invited to join the prominent law firm of Charles Hibbert Tupper and Wallace Graham. Charles Hibbert was the son of Sir Charles Tupper, one of the **Fathers of Confederation.** Robert continued to work extremely hard. Robert's lawyer friends, like his mother and his brother, thought that he worked too hard and was too serious, but he was gaining a reputation as a hard-working lawyer. A few short years later, Robert formed his own law firm with three partners. It became one of the largest in the Maritime provinces.

Robert Borden marries Laura Bond

In September 1889, Robert began 48 years of happy marriage by wedding **Laura Bond** whose father owned a Halifax hardware store. She was intelligent and energetic. Here was someone Robert could have fun with. Together they enjoyed playing tennis and golf. She involved Robert in her love of theatre and music. Although Robert worked very hard, he and Laura enjoyed travelling and took regular vacations.

Although Robert works very hard, he and Laura love the theatre; play golf and tennis together; and take regular vacations.

1882

One day, Robert opens a bottle of stout in the crowded compartment of an English train. Because the stout has been shaken by the movement of the train, it drenches everyone within range when it is opened. Two little children dance gaily and mirthfully under the cascade of beer. Their beautifully dressed mother gives Robert a horrified look, but she does accept his apology. An elderly farmer fares the worst. The stout hits him between the eyes and some even goes up his nose. The poor man mops up the stout with a huge red handkerchief and comments mildly, "Well, this is hard on a teetotaller."

17

When asked to to run for a seat in Parliament, Robert flatly refuses. Reluctantly, he reconsiders and wins a seat. When the Conservatives lose the election, Sir Wilfrid Laurier becomes PM and Robert and the rest of the Conservatives form the Opposition.

Robert dislikes politics and finds parliamentary debate more stressful than speaking in court. As a politician, he has two main problems. First, he does not have Laurier's charisma or skill as an orator. Second, his attempts to reconcile differences of opinion among his colleagues are often interpreted as indecisiveness.

Chapter 3

Some waste of time is inevitable

Sir John A. Macdonald became the first prime minister of Canada in 1867 and served until his death in 1891—except for five years during the 1870s. Following Sir John A.'s death, the Conservative Party fell into disarray because no strong leader was waiting in the wings to replace him. As a result, four different men served as Conservative prime ministers between 1891 and 1896. **Sir John Abbott** resigned due to ill health; **Sir John Thompson** died of a heart attack; and both **Sir Mackenzie Bowell** and Sir Charles Tupper were defeated over the **Manitoba Schools** issue.

Parliament and politics

Sir Charles Tupper persuaded Robert to run for the Conservative Party in the 1896 federal election. At first, he flatly refused. He had never even considered entering politics and wasn't even sure which party he really supported. But eventually, Tupper won him over. Reluctant as he was to run for **parliament**, Robert won his seat in the riding of Halifax. However, the Conservatives lost the 1896 election to the Liberal party led by Sir Wilfrid Laurier. Laurier became prime minister, and Robert went to Ottawa as a member of the Opposition.

1896
Robert is elected as a member of Parliament for Halifax.

1900
The Conservative party is defeated in the federal election.

Charles Tupper resigns as leader; Robert is offered the position but declines.

1901
Robert becomes leader of the Conservative party.

1904
Robert's office is damaged by fire.

He's defeated in the general election and loses his seat in Halifax.

1905
Robert wins a seat in Carleton, Ontario, and moves to Ottawa.

1911
Robert becomes the eighth prime minister of Canada.

He serves as president of the Privy Council.

There was much that Robert disliked about politics. He found parliamentary debate more stressful than speaking in court, and he was disappointed with the lack of dignity in the behaviour of members of Parliament. "Methods were unbusinesslike and waste of time enormous," he wrote, although he quickly concluded "that in parliamentary government waste of time is quite inevitable."

Robert leads the Opposition

In February 1901, Robert replaced Sir Charles Tupper as leader of the Conservative Party and spent the next 10 years rebuilding it. In 1905, Robert gave up his law practice to devote full time to politics, and he and his wife Laura moved permanently to Ottawa because his work kept him there most of the time.

In 1903, Robert, who did not speak French fluently, made his first speech in French. He said that the Liberals had not done enough for the country and that their motto could be *Pas encore* ("not yet"). He then asked a series of rhetorical questions about the Liberal record in Parliament. For example, "Have the Liberals reduced the rate of taxation?" And, "Have the Liberals reduced expenditures?" He answered each of his questions with the words "pas encore" and each time the audience shouted back enthusiastically, "pas encore." Because "pas encore" can mean either "not yet" or "not again," Robert finally began to wonder if the audience were really supporting him or if they were implying that his speech was too long—as in, "Isn't he ever going to stop talking?"

Immigration and racial intolerance

Prime Minister Laurier and his minister of the interior, **Clifford Sifton**, began to encourage large-scale immigration, mainly to western Canada. Most of the newcomers became farmers. Others became labourers in the mining, lumbering, or construction industries. A few moved to the cities. Between 1896 and 1911, nearly two-million people immigrated to Canada.

Most of the immigrants were English-speaking people from Britain or the United States. Others came from Europe, and about 40,000 came from Asia. Robert, like many Canadians at that time, held very strong racist views. They preferred that immigrants be white, English-speaking protestants, fearing that other immigrants would change Canadian society. As a result, stricter immigration laws were passed by the liberals between 1906 and 1910.

A Place Within the Empire

Canada and the rest of the world underwent dramatic changes in the first decade of the twentieth century. Canadian soldiers fought overseas for the first time in the **Boer War** in South Africa, and there was much political

Robert believed that politics was a responsibility, something that a successful man should take on in the public interest.

He never liked public speaking or debating. Although he did get used to them, he found them physically and emotionally demanding.

The Komagata Maru
and racial intolerance

One of the most shocking examples of racial intolerance in Canadian history occurred in May 1914. It became known as the incident of the *Komagata Maru*, and Robert would be a part of it.

Australia had implemented a "White Australia policy," restricting the immigration of non-white people. New Zealand quickly did the same. This had angered people in the British colony of India, and the British were concerned that it would affect their ability to govern the colony (which was already agitating for independence). Canada also wanted to stop Indian immigration but was warned by Britain not to. So, instead of a direct ban, Canada chose to implement the "continous journey" regulations of 1908. This devious legislation was designed to stop Indian newcomers by restricting any immigration that required a ship to make a detour in another country. As most ships from India stopped in Hong Kong, China, and Japan on their way to Vancouver, this would effectively crush their legal ability to come to the new dominion.

Gurdit Singh was a wealthy Indian businessman living in Singapore. He and many other veterans of the British Indian army decided to challenge the "continuous journey" legislation. As veterans of an army that had fought to defend the British Empire, they felt they had a right to settle in any part of the Empire that they had helped to maintain. So Singh chartered a ship to bring 374 people from the Punjab area of India and headed to Canada. The ship was called the *Komagata Maru*.

The ship got to the Vancouver port, and Canadian officials denied its inhabitants entry to Canada. One passenger told a British officer, "This ship belongs to the whole of India, this is a symbol of the honour of India, and if this was detained, there would be mutiny in the armies." Two months later, in July, with the ship occupants suffering from dehydration and starvation, Robert wrote that "the Hindus were endeavouring to procure arms from the United States and on the 19th [of July] I learned that they had resisted with great violence the attempt of our officers to board the ship."

The Canadian government ordered the naval cruiser HMCS *Rainbow* blow up the *Komagata Maru* if it did not leave Canadian waters immediately. On July 23, the ship was restocked with food and water and sent back to India.

Meanwhile, an immigration inspector and interpreter named William Hopkinson had been acting as an undercover agent for the Canadian government since 1907. Disguised with a turban and a false beard, he lived part-time as a Sikh labourer. In October 1914, after it became known that Hopkinson was a spy, he was shot and killed by a member of the Sikh community. His killer was tried and executed soon afterwards.

Communal fighting broke out in the Sikh community that had been split by the *Komagata Maru* and Hopkinson incidents. As a result, so many deaths occurred and so many people returned to India that only 700 Sikhs remained in Canada by 1918.

There was also violence in India. Twenty passengers of the *Komagata Maru* were killed and nine injured when a riot broke out after the British tried to divert the ship from landing in Calcutta, India. Gurdit Singh managed to escape and remained a fugitive until 1922, when Mahatma Gandhi urged him to give himself up. He served five years in jail in India and was celebrated as a true patriot of the Indian people for his efforts to fight injustice.

The "continuous journey" rule, however, remained in effect until 1947.

For more information about the *Komagata Maru*, visit our website at www.jackfruitpress.com.

unrest in both Europe and Asia. The main issue in the federal election of September 1911 was **reciprocity**, or free trade, with the United States. The Conservative's campaign slogan was "No truck nor trade with the Yankees." The Conservatives said that people who supported reciprocity were disloyal to Canada and Britain. Their campaign was helped by the speaker of the US **House of Representatives**, who said, "I hope to see the day when the American flag will float over every square foot of the British North American possessions clear to the North Pole."

In Quebec, the naval question was much more important than reciprocity. Prime Minister Laurier's Naval Service Act of 1910 created a small navy that would be under Canadian control, although Canadians could agree to make it available to the British in wartime. Both the Conservatives and the **Quebec nationalists** opposed the Naval Service Act, but for opposite reasons. The Conservatives thought that the Liberals had not done enough and that Canada should automatically provide a sizable fleet of warships for the British Navy on request. They dismissed Laurier's attempts, calling his a "tin-pot navy". The Quebec nationalists, on the other hand, feared that the Liberals had gone too far. The nationalists feared that pressure from English Canadians and the British might involve Canadian ships in foreign wars. Although the Quebec nationalists disagreed with the Conservatives, they cooperated with them to help defeat the Liberals in Quebec.

Winning the election

As a result of anti-reciprocity feelings across Canada and opposition to the Naval Services Act in Quebec, the Conservatives won the 1911 election. Robert Borden thus became prime minister of Canada with 134 Conservative seats compared to eighty-seven for the Liberals.

Robert wins the election and becomes the 8th prime minister of Canada! Robert and Laura are cheered by his Conservative colleagues.

Canada's minister of militia and defence, Sam Hughes, raises, trains and arms 33,000 soldiers within three months. But, at his insistence, the troops are equipped with Canadian-made supplies that are often unsuitable or poorly made.

Equipped with a Canadian-made rifle that frequently jams in wet and muddy conditions, our soldiers throw their own rifles away and pick up rifles from dead British soldiers whenever they can. Similar problems plague 23,000 shovels which turn out to be useless. Although the government has paid more than $30,000 for the shovels, all are later sold as scrap for $1,400. Hughes likely benefited from this deal because he was credited with inventing the shovel and its patent was issued in the name of his personal secretary.

Chapter 4

The war to end all wars

1914
Robert is knighted in England.

The War Measures Act is passed.

World War I begins.

1915
Robert visits wounded Canadian soldiers in British hospitals and on the frontlines.

Canadians fight their first major battles of World War I.

The Second Battle of Ypres takes place.

1916
Robert dismisses Sam Hughes, minister of militia.

World War I began on July 28, 1914, when Austria declared war on Serbia. Germany supported Austria. A few days later, on August 4, Britain, France, and Russia declared war on Germany. Because the countries within the **British Empire** did not have independent foreign policy, Canada and the other members of the Empire were automatically at war on the side of Britain. Sir Robert officially told Canadians that they were at war with Germany on August 18. At that time, he said, "We stand shoulder to shoulder with Britain and the other British **dominions** in this quarrel."

When the war broke out, the Canadian Parliament immediately passed the War Measures Act, giving the government authority to do anything it believed necessary to fight the war. The act allowed the government to control production of goods; to censor all forms of communication; to arrest and detain citizens without officially charging them; and to deport, without trial, people suspected of being enemy aliens.

Robert had no children of his own, but he was close to both his much-younger brother Henry (Hal) and his nephew Henry.

At the start of World War I, Canada was not well prepared to fight. The Canadian Navy consisted in two old **cruisers** that Canada had purchased from the British Royal Navy in 1910. These ships, along with their 350 officers and men, were offered to Great Britain to be placed at the disposal of His Majesty for general service in the Royal Navy. Just before the start of the war, British Columbia purchased two American submarines because they were worried that German ships might attack the British Columbian coast. Because the United States was officially neutral until it entered the war in 1917, selling the submarines to Canada was against American law. Thus, the submarines had to sneak out of American territorial waters. Sir Robert wrote that the two subs, which the Canada Navy agreed to pay for, "got away just ahead of the United States' order to detain them, and succeeded in evading United States' cruisers which pursued them."

The trouble with Sam Hughes

Sam Hughes had been minister of militia and defence since 1911. He was hard-working and well-qualified for the position, but he was also difficult to get along with. According to Sir Robert, Hughes showed excellent judgment half the time. The rest of the time his "conduct and speech were so eccentric as to justify the conclusion that his mind was unbalanced."

Within three months of the declaration of war, Hughes had raised, trained and armed 33,000 soldiers and accompanied them to Britain. That was considered excellent. Hughes insisted on using Canadian-made war supplies. That was also considered excellent. However, Hughes went too far. He insisted on using Canadian-made supplies even when they were unsuitable or made poorly. There were widespread accusations of corruption and incompetence against the two Canadian munitions factories which existed in 1914.

Both factories were located in Quebec City. One of the factories manufactured the Ross Rifle, developed by Sir Charles Ross and produced since 1903. It was a fine target rifle, but it frequently jammed when fired rapidly in wet and muddy conditions. Soldiers hated the Ross so much in battle that they would pick up rifles from dead British soldiers and throw their own rifles away. Finally Hughes was overruled by military leaders, and the Ross was replaced with English-made Lee-Enfield rifles.

Another example of unsuitable equipment that Hughes insisted on using was a spade with a hole in the centre that was meant as a combination shovel and shield against sniper bullets. Hughes ordered 23,000 of these tools, known as the MacAdam Shovel, at $1.35 each. They proved useless for digging and did almost nothing to protect soldiers from gunfire. Although the government paid more than $30,000 for the shovels, all 23,000 were later sold as scrap for $1,400. Hughes likely benefited from this deal because he was credited with inventing the shovel, although its patent was issued in the name of his personal secretary Ena MacAdam.

The causes of World War I

When the summer of 1914 began, nobody thought that the world was a few weeks away from a massive war. The murder of Franz Ferdinand, heir to the throne of Austria-Hungary, by Serbian terrorists on June 28 was not even viewed as a major crisis. But over the next few weeks, the European powers—France, Germany, Great Britain, and Russia—would set off a chain of actions and consequences, which would lead to millions of soldiers going to battle.

These European powers had successfully dealt with more serious issues in recent years without going to war, and their leaders believed that diplomacy would settle this matter quickly. Some of their leaders even continued their vacations. The **Austro-Hungarian** Empire, upset (but not too upset) over the death of its archduke, eventually decided to retaliate against the nation of Serbia, whom it believed had assisted the terrorists. While the Serbs were a small nation, unable to oppose their larger neighbour on their own, they could rely on the help of their ally, Russia. But if Russia decided to go to war against Austria-Hungary, the latter had Germany backing them up. And the Germans knew that if they went to war against Russia, it also meant that they were at war with France, who had made an alliance with Russia.

All the leaders understood this situation very well, and they would send messages to each other trying to figure a way out of this growing crisis. But at the same time, others were eager to go to war, including some of Germany's military leaders, who believed that it was necessary to make a pre-emptive strike against France and Russia before they became too

powerful. The Germans believed that they could quickly defeat the French, as they had in 1871, and then send their armies against the Russians. But their plan for invading France involved going through another country—Belgium.

On July 28, 1914, Austria-Hungary declared war on Serbia, and over the next few days the other European powers made their own declarations and mobilized their armies. For a few days, it seemed that Great Britain was not going to be involved in the war. But British leaders believed that the Germans would too easily defeat the French, and they worried this would damage their own interests. Therefore, on August 4, Great Britain declared war on Germany, saying that the Germans had broken a 75-year-old treaty not to invade Belgium. For historians this excuse sounds very hollow, since the British military commanders were also planning to attack Belgium if the Germans did not do so first. But it was very good propaganda for the British leaders to tell their people they were fighting to save the poor Belgian people. As for Canada, the reasons we went to war were more straightforward. Although Canada was its own nation, we were still part of the British Empire and our foreign policy was largely controlled by London. When Great Britain went to war, all of the British Dominions—including Canada, Newfoundland, Australia, New Zealand, South Africa, India—automatically were also at war. Eventually, more than 40 countries were involved in World War I, with battles being fought across the globe. Meanwhile, it was more than a year after the war started before actual fighting took place between Austria-Hungary and Serbia.

For more information about this topic, visit our website at www.jackfruitpress.com.

One of the most unpleasant jobs for the nurses was replacing the cotton sponges soaked in carbolic acid that were used to treat the soldiers' bullet and shell wounds. The acid also helped to prevent infection.

The soldiers called it the "Ceremony of the Plugs". It couldn't have been any nicer a "ceremony" for the soldiers than it was for the nurses.

The politics of war

By December 1914, Sir Robert believed that Canada and the other dominions should play a larger decision-making role in the conduct of the war. He travelled to Britain and France three times during the war where he consulted with British officials and visited Canadian soldiers on the front and in hospitals. During his 1915 visit, he complained to British colonial secretary **Bonar Law** and minister of munitions, **David Lloyd George** (who became prime minister the following year) that Canada was receiving insufficient information about important war issues. Lloyd George admitted that there had been problems with Britain's war preparations. Another minister spoke of the shortage of munitions and other goods, but he declared that the "chief shortage was of brains."

In 1915, Sir Robert visited wounded Canadians in fifty-two hospitals throughout England and France. He later wrote, "One's spirit was thrilled by their cheerfulness and heroism, but bruised by the realization of their suffering. As I passed through the long lines of hospital beds, every Canadian would raise himself as he saw me approaching and on his lips would be a smile, even if he were enduring intense pain."

Conditions did not improve. As Canadian soldiers fought and died in the mud of the trenches of the **western front**, Sir Robert became increasingly frustrated by the British government's unwillingness to consult the governments of the dominions before making important military decisions. In January 1916, Sir Robert wrote to the Canadian **high commissioner** in London, "Steps of the most important character have been taken without the slightest consultation with the authorities of this dominion ... Is this war being waged by the United Kingdom alone, or is it a war waged by the whole empire?"

Sam Hughes is finally fired

In 1915, Hughes established a Canadian headquarters in London to take command of all Canadian military activities overseas, and in 1916 he planned to move the militia department to England. Sir Robert criticized him for acting without cabinet authorization and overruled the militia plan. Sir Robert established the ministry of overseas forces instead and appointed **Sir George Perley** to lead it rather than Hughes. Hughes was furious and tried to overturn Sir Robert's decision. Finally Sir Robert had had enough, and he fired Sam Hughes in November 1916.

More trouble at home

On top of all the tragedies and problems of war, Canada suffered another tragedy on February 3, 1916. That evening, as Sir Robert was working in his office in the Parliament Building, someone yelled that the building was on fire. "We hurried out, and in the corridor leading to the reading

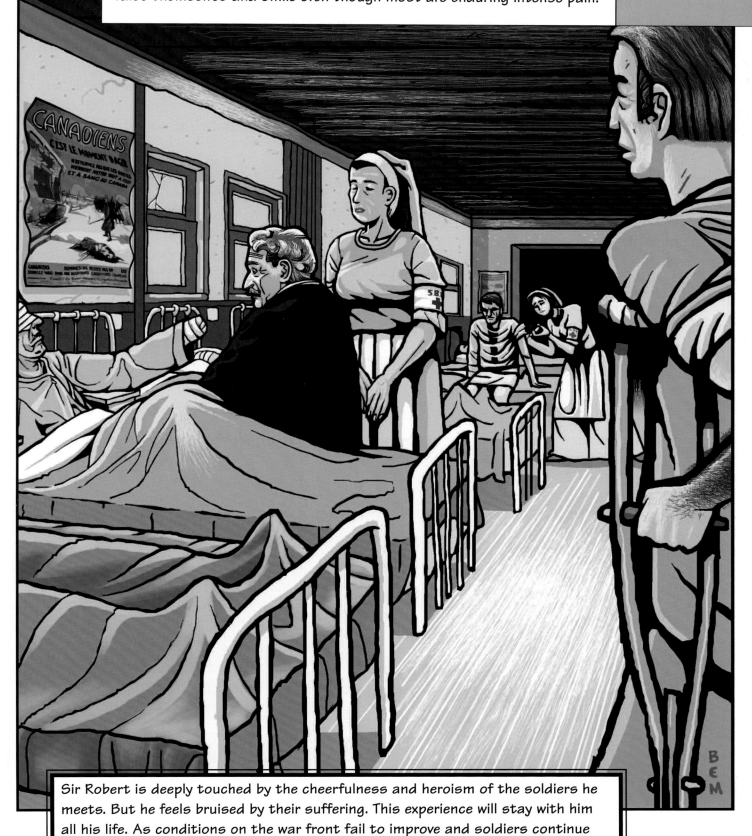

Visiting fifty-two hospitals in England and France, Sir Robert passes through long lines of hospital beds on which wounded Canadian soldiers raise themselves and smile even though most are enduring intense pain.

1915

Sir Robert is deeply touched by the cheerfulness and heroism of the soldiers he meets. But he feels bruised by their suffering. This experience will stay with him all his life. As conditions on the war front fail to improve and soldiers continue to fight and die in the trenches, the PM becomes ever more determined to do whatever he can to end the war. He feels he owes it to these young men.

In Sam Hughes' opinion, Robert is "a lovely fellow; very capable, but not a very good judge of men or tactics; and is gentle-hearted as a girl."

In Robert's opinion, Sam Hughes had an unbalanced mind!

room there was a great volume of thick black smoke through which darted long tongues of flame, accompanied by short, sharp sounds like explosions," he wrote in his autobiography.

The Parliament building was destroyed. Only the library was saved because the librarian had insisted upon iron fire doors being built between the centre block and the library. At the time of the fire, a clerk quickly ordered the doors shut. When Sir Robert went home shortly after midnight, the fire was still blazing fiercely. About an hour later the whole building collapsed.

The ruins were still smoking when Sir Robert returned the next morning. Seven people—one **member of Parliament**, two women visitors, three government employees, and a police officer—died in the fire. Because it was war time, many people thought that the fire was started by spies. But investigators found no evidence of sabotage. They concluded that the likely cause was careless smoking of a cigar, even though smoking was prohibited in the reading room where the fire began.

SAM HUGHES

The "war to end all wars" is drawing to a close. With US forces joining the Allies in 1917, the central powers are quickly crumbling. Exhausted and disheartened, German morale is dealt a further blow by the death of its greatest aerial ace, the Red Baron.

Manfred von Richthofen was a German pilot of aristocratic descent who downed more enemy planes than any other ace in World War I. Because of his habit of painting his airplane completely red, he came to be called the Red Baron. He was killed on April 21, 1919, while pursuing Canadian pilot, Wilfred "Wop" May.

1916

The Second Battle of Ypres is the first major action for Canadian troops and the first time that poison gas is used in the war. The French are unable to withstand the gas and are forced to retreat, but Canadian soldiers battle on.

The gas takes the soldiers by surprise—no one has gas masks. A Canadian soldier who had studied chemistry recognizes the yellow clouds as chlorine gas and orders the soldiers to pee on a handkerchief and hold it over their mouths and noses. The ammonia in urine neutralizes the gas and although unpleasant, many Canadian soldiers survive.

32

Chapter 5

Canada's unstoppable storm troopers

1917
Robert changes his constituency to King's County, Nova Scotia.

He attends the Imperial War Conference in May.

Canadians fight in the Battle of Vimy Ridge.

He announces the introduction of conscription (mandatory military service).

The conscription issue divides the country and Borden's cabinet. In response, Borden proposes the formation of a coalition government between the Conservative and Liberal parties, called the Unionist party.

The Unionist party wins the election of 1917.

1918
Robert travels to England to consult with war leaders.

With the war situation growing more desperate, British prime minister David Lloyd George knew he needed the dominions more than ever to win the war. In March 1917, Lloyd George invited the prime ministers of the British dominions—Canada, Australia, New Zealand, and South Africa—to attend meetings of an **Imperial War Cabinet** and an **Imperial War Conference** in London, England. Sir Robert was delighted. Here was the answer to his calls for more direct consultation about the running of the war. In addition to discussing the war, the prime ministers, led by Sir Robert and **Jan Smuts** of South Africa, would pass a resolution calling for a post-war conference to recognize the dominions as "autonomous nations of an imperial commonwealth" with the right to "an adequate voice in foreign policy and in foreign relations" and with "continuous consultation in all important matters of common Imperial concern." Sir Robert's vision of a more independent Canada was being realized.

War takes its toll

At home in Canada, relations between the Conservative government and the people of Quebec became progressively worse as the war dragged on—mainly over the issue of conscription which was strongly opposed by most French Canadians. Canada had relied entirely upon volunteer soldiers to fight the war until 1917. However by 1917, as more and more servicemen were killed or wounded in battle, it became increasingly difficult to attract enough volunteers to replace it looks like we've got the job of kicking Fritz out of Vimy Ridge. The French lost over 100,000 men trying to take that place. We hope to do better. At least all us Canadians are together and we've got Commander Currie looking out for us. Until he showed up, they were using us pretty poorly, now we get some fruit with our tea!

April 9, 1917

We're all nervous with zero hour coming up fast but after all the months of planning and training, everyone just wants it to be over with. Funny to think how this might be the last thing I ever write

April 13 - 1917

We did it! It was hell and I can't believe I lived through it. So many didn't. I saw so many acts of heroism that I've lost count. The French can't believe it and they've sent a load of champagne up to the new line to celebrate. We're still waiting for it. Everyone lost friends, so the guys are all pretty quiet, but everyone knows that we did well out there and

that Canadian troops might get a little respect now that we've proven ourselves. The other guys are already treating us differently. Even the cook, an old Brit named Edward, has stopped calling us "Bloody colonists." and sneaks us extra rum when the officers are not around.

For weeks the soldiers carefully planned and rehearsed the attack. The Canadians won, but over 10,000 soldiers were killed or wounded. They fought over an open graveyard—100,000 French soldiers were killed in a previous attempt to capture Vimy Ridge. The capture of Vimy Ridge is seen as a defining moment in Canadian history.

Nov. 1, 1917

Dearest Maggie,

I cannot tell you how much I miss you and our walks by the lake. I can't believe that I left your side to go live in a trench. You never want to smell a trench, Mags, it'd make you spew. And we pretty much live with thousands of rats! Some of the guys make pets of them and claim that if you watched them, they gave warning of an impending artillery attack. It's true, and I owe my life to these creatures many times over.

Since July, we've been slogging through a constant downpour of water and steel. We just took a village called Passchedaele after 3 months of terrible fighting. You never want to hear a machine gun, Mags. Or a gas alarm.

Our foul-tempered Sergeant caught a piece of iron in his liver and died a few days ago. None of us were very sorry until it came to light that a lot of things were done for our platoon that weren't done for anyone else, thanks to him. I hope my luck holds true and that I'll walk with you again sometime.

Love,
Allen

Soldiers fight in a swamp so deep that men and horses actually drown in it. Wireless radio, successfully used for the first time in battle, plays an important role in Canada's victory. Over 3,000 soldiers die and 13,000 are wounded or missing after thirteen days of fighting—all for the gain of seven kilometers of land that the British soon abandon.

Women won the right to vote in Canadian elections in 1917. They also won the right to run for political office.

Roberta MacAdams, a member of the Canadian Army Medical Corps, was elected to the Alberta legislature in September 1917 as a representative of the soldiers and military nurses from Alberta who were serving oversees.

Four years later, Agnes Campbell Macphail became the first woman elected to the Canadian parliament.

them. It was now taking almost four months to replace the men killed or wounded in one month. Earlier in the war Sir Robert had promised not to impose conscription, but now he had to face the fact that it might be necessary. He needed to make a difficult choice—one that would have serious consequences for all Canadians.

After attending military meetings in Britain and talking with wounded Canadian soldiers recuperating in British hospitals, Sir Robert promised the Imperial War Cabinet that Canada would increase her manpower contribution to the war. He also decided that conscription would be necessary to meet his commitment. On June 11, 1917, Sir Robert introduced the Military Service Act in the House of Commons. By that act, all males between 18 and 45 would be eligible for compulsory military service, although exceptions could be made. English-speaking Canadian were not unanimously in favour of conscription, but they were far more supportive than Quebecers. Quebec nationalists argued that Canada had no business fighting an imperialistic European war, and anti-government rallies protesting conscription were organized.

The conscription election of 1917

Because of the war, there had not been a federal election since 1911, although elections are supposed to be held at least every five years according to the Canadian Constitution. With the nation divided over conscription, Sir Robert proposed the formation of a coalition or national unity government of Liberals and Conservatives in order to put the Military Service Act into effect and to govern Canada for the remainder of the war. Liberal leader, Sir Wilfrid Laurier rejected the proposal because of opposition from Quebec members of his caucus and fears that Quebec nationalists would be able to exploit the situation for their political gain.

What happened next was a unique event in Canada's post-Conferderation history. On October 12, several pro-conscription Liberals crossed the floor of Parliament and joined Sir Robert. They agreed to form a new union government with a cabinet of twelve Conservatives; nine Liberals and independents; and one labour minister. Sir Robert then called an election for December 1917, running as head of the **Unionist party**. The only issue was conscription.

Two acts of Parliament, the Military Voters Act and the Wartime Elections Act, were passed before the election. By the Military Voters Act, conscientious objectors lost their right to vote. Also, members of the military could vote for a party rather than a candidate, and the votes could be distributed wherever they would best serve the party. This provision directly resulted in Unionist victories in fourteen ridings. The Wartime Elections Act disenfranchised people born in an enemy country who had become

Conscription

Some people might say that World War I united Canada. In reality, it divided us, pitting English Canada against French Canada. The issue was conscription—forcing men to join the army and go to Europe to fight in the trenches. It was one of the most difficult problems for Robert Borden to deal with, and historians still debate whether he made the right decision.

At first, it seemed that Canada would not need to compel anyone to join the army. Young men were volunteering by the thousands and, for the first couple of years, there was a steady stream of new recruits arriving in Europe. By the end of 1916, over 300,000 Canadians had volunteered to take part in the war, an impressive number considering that the country's population was only eight million.

But nearly all of the support for the war was coming from English Canada, especially from British-born Canadians. These people truly believed that they were fighting not only to defend the British Empire, but to save the poor French and Belgian peoples from alleged atrocities being committed by the Germans.

Meanwhile, in French-speaking Canada, there was no eagerness for this war, or for joining it. Quebec journalists saw it as a fight between imperial powers that did not concern them. An isolationist view had developed among French Canadians, and they believed they should not get involved in foreign wars. Furthermore, many French Canadians were deeply upset that the government of Ontario was closing its French schools and imposing English-only education. French Canadians asked how it was that Canada was fighting to stop oppression in Europe while at the same time oppressing their own minority at home.

As the war continued, willingness to join the army decreased among all Canadians. News reports described how terrible life was on the front lines and the list of the dead was growing. By the spring of 1917, the Canadian army was increasing by only 4,000 men per month—far below what was needed to replace casualties. After a visit to Europe, where Borden saw for himself how desperate the situation was, the prime minister decided to use conscription.

French-Canadian politicians urged the government not to go through with this plan and the federal election later that year was mainly about that issue. But Borden was able to win the election, largely on the support from English Canada and from the votes of troops serving overseas.

In the end, about 24,000 conscripts served on the front lines of Europe. The military impact of these troops was debatable, but the social and political impact of conscription was deep and long-lasting. It included greater distrust between English and French Canada, with the latter group becoming more isolationist. Robert Borden's Conservative party would find little support in Quebec for decades afterwards; residents of that province did not easily forget who it was that had forced their sons to fight and die in a war they wanted no part of.

For more information about this topic, visit our website at www.jackfruitpress.com.

On December 6, 1917 two ships collided in the Halifax harbour and one was full of munitions. The ship exploded, creating the largest explosion until the atomic age of the 1940s.

Within minutes, the explosion created a tsunami that rose up to eighteen metres and washed the other ship onto the shore where it was stranded until spring.

To make matters worse, a major blizzard hit that night. Many bodies were not discovered until the following spring.

Over 2,000 people died, 9,000 were injured and 6,000 people were left completely homeless. Thousands of others had to survive the winter in their damaged homes

As you can imagine, many people thought that Germans had attacked the city, but the Halifax explosion was caused by the negligence of the captains of both ships.

Canadian citizens or British subjects after 1902. The Unionist party won the election by 153 seats to the Liberals' eighty-two. Quebec elected sixty-two Liberals and only three Unionists, causing a serious rift between Quebec and the rest of Canada.

Women win the right to vote

World War I and the 1917 election brought about an important social change for Canadian women. They won the right to vote in federal elections for the first time. The Military Voters Act gave the vote to the over 3,000 women who served as nurses in the Canadian Army Medical Corps. And the Wartime Elections Act gave the right to vote to wives, widows, mothers, sisters, or daughters of anyone serving in Canada's military.

Earlier in his political life, Sir Robert may not have actually wanted to give women the right to vote. In a speech he gave to the **Women's Canadian Club** in Montreal in 1910, he merely stated that women should involve themselves in politics. Sir Robert told his audience that it was the duty of women as well as men to make Canadian political parties stronger by working hard to support them.

By 1917, Sir Robert was in favour of votes for women, saying "The franchise will be extended to women, not chiefly in recognition of devoted and capable service in the war, but as a measure of justice too long delayed." It is also true that Sir Robert gave women the right to vote in order to help elect his Unionist government. He knew that women serving in the medical corps and the female relatives of men serving in the military would almost certainly support conscription and thus vote for the Unionists.

Violence at home

December 6, 1917, was a day like no other in Canadian history. The harbour in the city of Halifax, Nova Scotia, literally exploded, killing and maiming thousands of people. When Sir Robert learned about the tragic explosion, he rushed to Halifax and telegraphed Ottawa to send $500,000 in immediate aid. The following spring, violence of a different sort exploded in Quebec.

In the spring of 1918, an anti-conscription riot broke out in Quebec City. When Quebec police refused to intervene, the federal government sent troops who opened fire, killing four innocent people. By 1918, however, it was not only French Canadians who opposed conscription. Many farmers and labour leaders did so as well. Labour leaders demanded that all war profiteering end before conscription be imposed, and farmers argued that they should be exempt from military service because food production was essential to the war effort.

The Battle of the Somme is one of the bloodiest battles in human history. Over one million people are killed or injured during the battles, which take place in summer and autumn.

British PM, Lloyd George said that the Canadians played such an important role at the Somme that "for the remainder of the war they were brought along to head the assault in one great battle after another. Whenever the Germans found the Canadian Corps coming into line, they prepared for the worst".

The British Empire suffered almost one million deaths in battle during the First World War, and twice that many were wounded.

Over 60,000 of these deaths were Canadian men and fifty-six were Canadian nurses, working on the front lines.

The war also took its toll on Sir Robert. He wrote in his diary in the summer of 1919, "For several weeks I had kept on my feet with great difficulty, as I was suffering severely from exhaustion, resulting from the strain and anxiety... and from the constant and intense labours imposed on me."

Ironically, the military importance of conscription was negligible. Only 24,000 Canadian conscripts ever saw action in the war. However, the crisis over conscription left many Canadians divided over politics and distrustful of government.

Facing off with Lloyd George

When Sir Robert went to England in the spring of 1918 to attend the second session of the Imperial War Cabinet, he took his 16-year-old nephew **Henry Borden** along as an unpaid secretary. Henry recounted an incident which took place when the members of the war cabinet were discussing the conduct of the war at the British prime minister's weekend residence. Sir Robert turned to Lloyd George, pointed his finger at him, and said in a voice shaking with emotion, "Mr. Prime Minister, I want to tell you that, if ever there is a repetition of the battle of Passchendaele, not a Canadian soldier will leave the shores of Canada so long as the Canadian people entrust the government of their country to my hands."

Sir Robert strongly criticized recent British conduct of the war in a speech to the Imperial War Cabinet. He told the cabinet that **General Currie**, leader of the Canadian forces, stated that British military intelligence was so poor that Currie always tore up documents sent by the Chief (British) Intelligence Office without reading them because he knew the information was more likely to mislead than help him lead his troop in battle. Sir Robert went on to say that incompetent British officers were not removed from their posts. "Officers who make mistakes are always ready to atone by their death in fighting to the last, but mistakes . . . will end in losing this war."

Sir Robert concluded that the outcome of the war depended on how quickly the American troops (who did not enter the war until April 1917) could be "organized, trained, and put into the fighting line."

Only six months later the **Allies** did win the war which ended officially at 11:00 a.m. on November 11, 1918. When the war ended, Sir Robert Laird Borden was aboard a ship en route to England.

The Hundred Days

In the spring of 1918, the war was going badly for the Allies. The Germans had begun Operation Michael, a massive attack against the British and French lines. Using speed, skill, and surprise, German storm troopers hoped they could break through these lines and capture the French capital of Paris. They wanted to deliver a knockout blow, and many believed they were about to win in March and April of 1918.

Hundreds of thousands were killed or wounded on both sides, and many Allied units were captured or forced to retreat. At first, the Germans made some rapid gains, taking back much of the land they had lost in recent years; but the progress of their soldiers soon slowed down. The British and French troops did suffer a defeat, but they were not shattered as the German commanders had hoped they would be.

Although the situation looked desperate for the Allies, it was the Germans who now were in trouble. Because of Allied blockades, German soldiers were short of food and medicine, and they suffered the most when influenza struck Europe. Germany did not have enough young men to replace their casualties, nor could they rely on Austria-Hungary and their other partners to assist them. Meanwhile, the Allies were actually getting stronger. Hundreds of thousands of fresh American soldiers had been arriving in Europe since the United States joined the war a year earlier. This allowed the Allies to stop the German advance, and then (in August, 1918) to go back on the offensive.

On August 8, the Allies began their attacks on the German positions—the first move in what would be called the Hundred Days. It was really a string of battles where Allied forces defeated and pushed back their German rivals.

The Canadian forces played a prominent role in these events. The Canadians had not been attacked during the German offensives earlier in the year, so they were in relatively good condition to lead attacks on the enemy lines. At places like Arras, Amiens, Valenciennes, and Canal du Nord, the Canadians won major victories, although these victories came with more than 40,000 casualties.

By October, the German leaders knew that they had lost, and that to continue fighting would be futile. It took just a few more weeks before their government collapsed, their ruler fled the country, and their remaining politicians signed an armistice agreement ending the war. The guns fell silent and the war officially ended at 11:00 a.m. on November 11—the 11th day of the 11th month of the year. The fortunes of war, which months earlier seemed to favour the Germans, had ended with the victory going to Canada and the Allies.

For more information about this topic, visit our website at www.jackfruitpress.com.

41

1919

Sir Robert insists that Canada be involved in negotiations of the peace treaty with Germany. But Britain's PM only wants to allow Canada to be present at sessions dealing with matters of direct Canadian concern.

Sir Robert is furious. He insists that Canada is entitled to participate in all the sessions. Eventually, Britain gives in and agrees to let its dominions (Canada, New Zealand, and Australia) have a say. This move marks the beginning of a whole new relationship between Canada, Britain and the rest of the British Empire.

Chapter 6

Peace and retirement

World War I was catastrophic, but it did have at least one positive effect for Canada. As Desmond Morton, a Canadian historian, wrote, "The emergence of Canadian sovereignty was the one great Canadian victory of the war."

Before 1914, the dominions of the British Empire did not have any say in international affairs. Now Sir Robert insisted that the Dominion leaders should be involved, along with the British, in the **Paris Peace Conference** which was called in January 1919 to negotiate the terms of peace after Germany lost the war.

Still, British prime minister David Lloyd George suggested that Canada, like smaller European countries such as Belgium and Portugal, only participate at the Paris Peace Conference when a matter of direct concern to them was discussed. Sir Robert was furious. The major powers—Britain, France, the United States, Italy, and Japan—were entitled to each have five delegates present at all sessions, and Sir Robert insisted that Canada was also entitled to be at all the sessions. "Canada," he said, "had lost more men killed in France than Portugal had put in the field." The Canadian government supported Sir Robert. They said that the Canadian people would not appreciate five American delegates sitting throughout the whole conference and no Canadians entitled to do so. Canada had been in the war since the beginning while the United States did not join until 1917. Moreover, Canada's views on the shape of a new Europe after the war needed to be heard.

Sir Robert did not spend all his time in Paris at the Peace Conference. One day he attended a baseball game played by Canadian soldiers. During the game, the ball was knocked into the crowd of spectators and a rather long and noisy argument about the rules of the game

1918
Robert attends the Paris Peace Conference.

He's appointed chancellor of McGill University.

1919
The Treaty of Versailles is signed on June 28, officially ending World War I.

1920
Robert resigns as prime minister.

Arthur Meighen becomes the ninth prime minister of Canada.

Canada joins the League of Nations.

1921
Robert attends the Washington Naval Disarmament Conference.

1930
He is appointed head of Canadian delegation to the League of Nations Society and Chairman of the Canadian Institute of International Affairs.

1937
Robert dies in Ottawa on June 10.

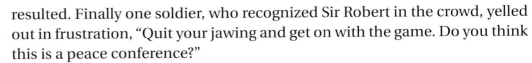

Sir Robert enjoyed his requirement, making up for 40 years of almost constant work. He took his first airplane ride at the age of 78 and made his final trip to Europe at the age of 82.

Shortly before his death, he instructed his nephew Henry that he wished to be remembered as "just plain Robert".

resulted. Finally one soldier, who recognized Sir Robert in the crowd, yelled out in frustration, "Quit your jawing and get on with the game. Do you think this is a peace conference?"

A treaty, a league, and retirement

On June 28, 1919, the Paris Peace Conference ended with the signing of the **Treaty of Versailles**. Sir Robert signed for Canada. The British government also agreed that the dominions and India should be given separate representation in the newly formed **League of Nations**, the first international organization of governments formed to promote peace and discuss international issues. Sir Robert fought and won a second battle to have the dominions also included as members of the **International Labour Organization**, which was formed as a separate agency of the league.

On July 19, 1920, Sir Robert retired as prime minister at the age of 66. He had never really enjoyed politics. Shortly after his retirement he wrote in his diary, "Democracy is always ungrateful, forgetful and neglectful. I am very happy to have given up my public duties and to have retired from public life." His health had suffered because of the strain of leading Canada through the war and the peace settlement. He was not a person who enjoyed controversy or arguments. His fights at home with Sam Hughes and over the conscription issue took a heavy toll on him—as did his efforts to gain Canada an international voice during and after the war.

He soon recovered his health and spent a long and busy retirement. He represented Canada at international conferences and served as president or chairman of a number of important Canadian organizations dedicated to

international affairs. At the 1926 Imperial Conference, a meeting which Sir Robert did not attend, the dominions were defined as "autonomous communities within the British Empire, equal in status, in no way subordinate one to another in any aspect of their domestic or external affairs, though united by common allegiance to the Crown, and freely associated as members of the British Commonwealth of Nations." Sir Robert lived to see this definition finally become law in Canada in 1931.

He lectured at universities, wrote several books, and enjoyed himself. He wrote, "I was very fond of outdoor life, but for nearly forty years I almost entirely gave it up." Now he had more time for cycling and playing golf, gardening, and fishing.

Sir Robert didn't take his first airplane ride until he was 78 years old. He enjoyed the trip so much that he decided to charter a plane to travel from Ottawa to his summer cottage at Echo Beach—a 30-minute trip by air. He soon gave up the idea, however, when he learned it would cost over $180 to make the trip.

A genuinely humble guy
Sir Robert died in Ottawa on June 10, 1937, at the age of 83. He and Laura had no children, but he was close to his nephew Henry. Shortly before his death, he instructed Henry, "Remember, Henry, none of this Sir stuff at the cemetery, just plain Robert Laird Borden."

Sir Robert Borden:

Sir Robert Borden's greatest achievement and greatest failure in politics both grew directly out of World War I. By the end of the war—largely due to his actions—Canada and the other British dominions had separate voices at the Paris Peace Conference and had made a major step toward becoming sovereign nations. Before World War I, Sir Robert was a staunch imperialist. Most Canadians of his time— especially if they were of British origin—strongly believed Canadians should be subjects of the British Empire. While he never fully lost his convictions, Sir Robert's direct witness of the politics of war changed him and Canada. You could say that under the leadership of Prime Minister Borden, Canada "grew up" as a country.

On the other hand, Sir Robert's handling of the conscription crisis of 1917

Canada's low-key hero

seriously damaged Canadian unity, causing a rift between Quebec and the rest of Canada that has never been completely healed. Another important legacy—giving women the vote in the 1917 federal election—is somewhat tarnished because it is so closely connected with the issue of conscription.

Yet, we admire many of Sir Robert's qualities as a person and sympathize with his shortcomings. Sir Robert was a self-made man. He became a successful lawyer and politician because of his dedication, intelligence, and hard work. His writing and public speaking were awkward and stilted, and he did not enjoy these very necessary aspects of his position as a political leader.

Sir Robert's racial intolerance would be completely unacceptable in a political leader today, and he can be strongly criticized for it. At the same time, however, we must realize that a large percentage of the population agreed with him and the standards of his time must be taken into account in judging him.

Whatever Sir Robert's faults, they cannot take away his achievement in giving Canada an independent voice in the world.

Timeline: The life and times of Sir Robert Borden

YEAR	ROBERT'S LIFE	EVENTS IN CANADA AND THE WORLD
1854	Robert is born in Grand Pré, Nova Scotia, on June 26.	Reciprocity begins between British North America and the United States. The Crimean War takes place in the Balkans and Crimean Peninsula: Russia fights the Ottoman (Turkish) Empire and its allies (Britain, France, and Sardinia) Many soldiers die needlessly due to terrible hospital conditions before Florence Nightingale introduces modern nursing methods.
1855		Bytown is renamed Ottawa.
1856		The Second Opium War takes place: China fights Britain and France in an attempt to end the opium trade.
1857		Ottawa becomes the new capital of the Province of Canada. The Revolt of 1857: India fights for freedom from British rule. The issues are laws that keep Indians impoverished and British army violations of the religious customs of Hindu and Muslim soldiers.
1859		Abraham Shadd became the first black person elected to public office.
1860		Construction begins on the House of Commons in Ottawa. The Maori Wars begin: The Maori of New Zealand fight to keep their land from British settlers. Large areas of land are confiscated, causing permanent damage to Maori society. The US Civil War begins: President Lincoln and the northern states want to abolish slavery. The southern states go to war against the North. The North wins and slavery is ended.
1863	Robert goes to Acacia Villa Academy.	
1866		Several Fenian raids take place on the border with the United States.
1867		Canadian Confederation takes effect on July 1. John A. Macdonald becomes the first prime minister of Canada.
1868	Robert becomes assistant school master in classical studies. He teaches in Horton, Nova Scotia.	The first Federal Militia Act creates the first Canadian army.
1870		The Red River Rebellion takes place. Thomas Scott is executed by Louis Riel's provisional government. The Northwest Territories and Manitoba are created.
1871		Construction of the Canadian Pacific Railway begins. British Columbia joins Confederation.
1872	Robert travels to the United States. He teaches in Matawan, New Jersey.	The first nationwide labour protest is held in Canada. Asian and native peoples are banned from voting in BC.
1873		Sir John A. Macdonald is forced to resign as prime minister because of the Pacific Scandal. Alexander Mackenzie becomes the second prime minister. The Northwest Mounted Police is formed.
1874	Robert returns to Nova Scotia. Robert works as an articled clerk in Robert Weatherbe and Wallace Graham's law office.	Liberals win a majority government in the federal election of January 22.

More on the life and times of Sir Robert Borden

YEAR	ROBERT'S LIFE	EVENTS IN CANADA AND THE WORLD
1875		The Supreme Court of Canada is established. The Indian Act is passed.
1876		
1877	He passes his final law exam.	Manzo Nagano is the first official Japanese immigrant to Canada. The Russian-Turkish War begins: a continuation of a series of wars between Russia and the Ottoman Empire over land boundaries.
1878	Robert is called to the Nova Scotia bar.	John A. Macdonald is elected for a second term as prime minister. The Canada Temperance Act is passed.
1879	Robert practises law with a partner, John T. Ross.	The Anglo-Zulu War takes place in South Africa: Britain wins and takes over control of Zululand. The War of the Pacific begins: Peru, Bolivia, and Chile fight over borders and natural resources.
1880	Robert works in a partnership in Kentville, Nova Scotia.	Edward Hanlan, a rower, becomes Canada's first world sports champion. Emily Stowe becomes Canada's first female doctor.
1882	Robert joins the prominent law firm of Tupper and Graham.	
1883		The Sino-French War starts: France and China fight over Vietnam. In the end, Vietnam is divided. China controls the north, France gets the south.
1885		The Canadian Pacific Railway is completed. Canada's first national park is created in Banff, Alberta. The Northwest Rebellion takes place. Riel is hanged for treason. The federal government imposes a head tax of $50 on Chinese immigrants.
1887	He makes his first appearance in the Supreme Court.	
1888	Robert visits England and France.	The Fisheries Treaty is passed. The first election takes place in the Northwest Territories.
1889	Robert marries Laura Bond on September 25.	
1890	He is made senior partner in his law firm.	
1891		Sir John A. Macdonald dies while in office. John Abbott becomes the third prime minister of Canada.
1892		Sir John Sparrow David Thompson becomes the fourth prime minister of Canada. The Criminal Code of Canada is established.
1893	Robert travels to London with his wife.	An international tribunal decides that Canadians have the right to hunt seals in the Bering Sea. The Stanley Cup is awarded for the first time to the Montreal Amateur Athletic Association hockey club, champions of the Amateur Hockey Association of Canada.
1894		Sir Mackenzie Bowell becomes the fifth prime minister of Canada.

49

Still more on the life and times of Sir Robert Borden

YEAR	ROBERT'S LIFE	EVENTS IN CANADA AND THE WORLD
1896	Robert is elected as a member of Parliament for Halifax.	Sir Charles Tupper becomes the sixth prime minister of Canada. Sir Wilfrid Laurier becomes the seventh prime minister.
1897		The Klondike gold rush occurs. Clara Brett Martin becomes the first woman admitted the Ontario bar. Queen Victoria celebrates her diamond (60th) jubilee.
1898		The Yukon Territory is formed. Spanish-American War takes place: Spain loses control over Cuba, Puerto Rico, the Philippine islands, Guam, and other islands.
1899		The South African War (Boer War) begins (1899-1902): The British win control of what is now the Republic of South Africa. The first Canadian troops are sent to the South African War.
1900	Robert is offered leadership of the Conservative party, but declines.	The Canadian government raises the head tax on Chinese immigrants to $100. Boxer Rebellion of China erupts. The Commonwealth of Australia is formed.
1901	He accepts leadership of the Conservative party, becoming leader of the Opposition.	Queen Victoria dies.
1902	Robert takes a political tour of the western provinces.	
1904	His office is damaged by fire on January 8. He loses in the general election and loses his seat in Halifax.	The Russo-Japanese War begins: Russia recognizes Japan as the dominant power in Korea and turns over some leased land in the Asian Pacific to Japan. The Trans-Siberian Railway is completed.
1905	He runs for the Carleton, Ontario, seat in a by-election and wins. He moves to Ottawa.	Alberta and Saskatchewan become provinces. The Russian revolution occurs: Russians protest against the government of Tsar Nicholas II.
1910		The Canadian Navy is created.
1911	Robert becomes the eighth prime minister of Canada. He serves as president of the Privy Council.	
1914	Robert is knighted in England.	The War Measures Act is passed. World War I begins on August 4.
1915	Robert visits wounded Canadian soldiers in British hospitals and on the frontlines.	The first major battle is fought by Canadians during World War I. Known as the Battle of Ypres, in Belgium, it lasts from April 22 to May 25.
1916	He dismisses Sam Hughes as minister of militia.	Manitoba amends its Election Act to allow women to vote in provincial elections.
1917	Robert attends the Imperial War Conference in May. He proposes the formation of the Union party, a coalition government between the Conservative and Liberal parties.	The conscription crisis occurs. Canadians fight in the Battle of Vimy Ridge in France. A temporary income tax is introduced. The National Hockey League (NHL) is formed. The Russian revolution ends with the Bolsheviks seizing power. The Union party wins the election of 1917.

Even more on the life and times of Sir Robert Borden

YEAR		ROBERT'S LIFE	EVENTS IN CANADA AND THE WORLD
1918		Robert travels to England to consult with war leaders. He attends the Paris Peace Conference. He becomes chancellor of McGill University (1918–1920).	White women are allowed to vote and are eligible to be candidates in all provinces except Prince Edward Island and Quebec. World War I ends on Armistice Day, November 11. A worldwide influenza epidemic breaks out and kills an estimated 25 million people between 1918 and 1919.
1919		Robert returns to Canada from Europe.	The Winnipeg General Strike occurs from May 15 to June 26. The Treaty of Versailles officially ends World War I.
1920		Robert resigns as prime minister.	The League of Nations is established and Canada joins. Arthur Meighen becomes the ninth prime minister. Women become eligible to sit in the House of Commons. The Progressive party forms. The RCMP takes over federal law enforcement.
1921		Robert serves as Canada's representative at the Conference on the Limitation of Armament in Washington, DC.	William Lyon Mackenzie King becomes the tenth prime minister of Canada. Agnes Macphail is the first woman elected to Parliament.
1922		Robert publishes *Canadian Constitutional Studies*.	The Chanak Affair takes place: Mackenzie King delays sending support for British troops in Turkey, insisting it be Parliament's decision. White women are allowed to vote in Prince Edward Island. The Union of Soviet Socialist Republics (USSR) is created.
1924		Robert becomes chancellor of Queen's University, in Kingston, Ontario (1924–1930).	The first national postal strike in Canada takes place.
1926			Arthur Meighen begins his second term. Old-age pension is introduced.
1928		Robert is named president of Crown Life Insurance.	
1929		Robert becomes president of Barclay's Bank. He publishes *Canada in the Commonwealth*.	The British Privy Council declares Canadian women to be legally "persons." The New York stock market crash triggers the Great Depression.
1930		He serves as president of the Canadian Historical Association and as Canada's chief delegate at the Assembly of the League of Nations.	Richard Bedford Bennett becomes the 11th prime minister. Cairine Wilson is the first appointed female senator. Pluto, the ninth planet in the solar system, is discovered.
1932			Co-operative Commonwealth Federation (CCF) party is founded.
1933			Adolf Hitler is appointed chancellor of Germany.
1935			The Bank of Canada is formed. The RCMP stops the On-to-Ottawa Trek in Regina. Tommy Douglas wins a seat in the CCF party's first election.
1936			The Canadian Broadcasting Corporation (CBC) is created. The Spanish Civil War begins.
1937		Sir Robert Borden dies on June 10 in Ottawa. He is buried in Beechwood Cemetery, Ottawa.	

Glossary: words and facts you might want to know

Abbott, Sir John (1821–1893): lawyer, professor, and Canada's third prime minister (1891–1892). He took over the position of PM when Sir John A. Macdonald died. He turned over the government to Sir John S.D. Thompson the following year. He was the first PM to be born in Canada. He was also mayor of Montreal from 1887 to 1889.

Acadians: French people who lived in the French colony of Acadia. Acadia included what is now Nova Scotia, Prince Edward Island and parts of New Brunswick and Quebec. Acadians began to arrive from France in the early 1600s to take part in the very profitable fur trade. In 1713, France lost control of Acadia to Great Britain. The British wanted to make sure that the Acadians would be loyal to them and demanded that they take an oath of allegiance. The Acadians refused and so in 1755 the British removed them from their homes and land. They were shipped down to the Thirteen Colonies (now the east coast of the USA) and Louisiana. It is estimated that 11 000 Acadians were deported between 1755 and 1762, when the deportations stopped.

Allies: term used to describe all the countries that fought against the Axis countries during World War II. The allied countries included Great Britain, France, the USA, the Soviet Union, and Canada. The Axis was an alliance between Germany, Italy, and, later, Japan.

Austro-Hungarian Empire: also known as Austria-Hungary, a country in Central Europe from 1867 to 1918. Within this country there were two parliaments, one in Austria and one in Hungary. There was also a central government that had responsibility for areas such as the navy, the army, and foreign policy. Following its defeat in World War I, the country was divided up into Austria and Hungary, in addition to land being given to other new and existing countries.

bar exams: the test that people have to pass to be allowed to practise law. "Bar" refers to the official organization of barristers (the British word for lawyers who can appear in court). Law students go to university, article (apprentice in a law firm), and then write the bar examination. When they complete all these steps, they are "called to the bar" which means they can start practising law.

Boer War (1899–1902): also known as the South African War. In a quest to acquire control of gold mines, the British took over two independent states in South Africa: South African Republic (Transvaal) and Orange Free State. Canada fought in the war at the request of Great Britain. Many Canadians, especially French Canadians, did not agree with sending Canadian soldiers to participate.

Bond, Laura (1863–1940): wife of Sir Robert Borden. They were married in 1889 and had no children. She is said to have been lively and attractive with interests in music and theatre. She and her husband also enjoyed playing tennis and golf.

Borden, Henry (1901–1989): nephew of Sir Robert Borden. He trained to be a lawyer and served in the federal government during World War II. He edited two books that were written by his uncle: *Memoirs* (1938) and *Letters to Limbo* (1971).

Bowell, Sir Mackenzie (1823–1917): born in Great Britain, he was Canada's fifth prime minister (1894–1896). As a Senator, he became prime minister upon the death of Sir John Thompson. He was forced to resign by his own Cabinet because of his inability to deal effectively with the Manitoba Schools Question.

British Empire: an old term that refers to Great Britain, all of its dependent countries and provinces, and the British dominions in the world.

classical studies: learning about ancient Greek and Roman worlds through the examination of their arts and literature, religion, history, and government.

More words and facts you might want to know

Conservative Party of Canada: the first party to govern the Dominion of Canada. It began in 1854 when politicians from Upper and Lower Canada joined to form a coalition government of the Province of Canada. It was initially called the Liberal-Conservative Party but changed its name to the Conservative Party when a separate Liberal Party was formed at the time of Confederation. Sir John A. Macdonald was its first leader.

cruiser: large, fast warship with less armour and firepower than a battleship. It was often used to go ahead of the rest of the fleet to look for the enemy.

Currie, General Arthur William (1875–1933): because of his successful leadership during the early part of World War I, he was the first Canadian to be appointed General of the Canadian Army during the final battles of 1918.

dominions: self-governing states of the British Empire (or later, the British Commonwealth). Prior to being a dominion, the state would have been a colony of Great Britain.

Fathers of Confederation: all of the people who represented the British North American colonies at one or more of the three conferences that paved the way for the Canadian confederation. The conferences were held in Charlottetown, Quebec and London, England between 1864 and 1867. Thirty-six parliamentary delegates attended one or more of them.

high commissioner: senior diplomat from one country who acts as a high ranking representative in another country.

House of Representatives: the lower part of the United States Congress. The upper part is called the Senate. Members of the House represent every state, with some states having more than one representative, depending on their population. Laws are proposed and voted on in the House.

Hughes, Sir Samuel (1853–1921): controversial minister of militia and defence before and during World War I (1911–1916). The equipment that he chose to outfit the Canadian army was often faulty. He was known for acting without asking for permission. He was forced to resign as minister by Sir Robert Borden.

Imperial War Cabinet: initiated in 1917, the group of prime ministers and other senior ministers from Great Britain and her dominions who gathered to agree on the British Empire's plan for the current war. It was created by British Prime Minister David Lloyd George.

Imperial War Conference: meetings that took place on alternate meeting days of the Imperial War Cabinet to discuss matter of interest to the British Empire, but not necessarily about the war. It was during these meetings that Borden requested that the dominions be able to dictate their own foreign policies and not be expected to follow Great Britain's policies.

International Labour Organization: agency of the United Nations that promotes safe and decent work environments for workers. It promotes fair wages, job security, productive work, and protection for injustice.

Laurier, Sir Wilfrid (1841–1919): Canada's 7th prime minister and the first one who was a French Canadian.

Law. Andrew Bonar (1858–1923): political partner of British Prime Minister David Lloyd George during World War I.

League of Nations: international organization that was formed after World War I in an attempt to prevent further wars between nations. It proved incapable of stopping World War II, its prime goal for existence. It was replaced by the United Nations Organization after World War II.

Liberal Party of Canada: the second party to govern the Dominion of Canada. The party was formed in 1867 after Canada's Confederation. Canada's second prime minister was a Liberal, Sir Alexander Mackenzie.

Lloyd George, David (1863–1945): British politician and prime minister (1916–1922). He helped guide Great Britain and the British Empire during World War I.

More words and facts you might want to know

Macdonald, Sir John Alexander (1815–1891): Canada's first prime minister (1867–1873, 1878–1891). Born in Scotland, he moved to Upper Canada with his family in 1820. He trained and worked as a lawyer before becoming involved in politics. He spent many years working on bringing the Province of Canada and the Maritime provinces together. On July 1, 1867 his dream came true with the creation of the Dominion of Canada. He died while in office in Ottawa.

Manitoba Schools Question: the debate about if Manitoba should have publicly funded Catholic schools in addition to the non-denominational (non-religious) public schools. When the province formed in 1870, both types of schools were paid for by public money. In 1890, the provincial government ended support of the Catholic schools. The federal government had the power to restore the Catholic schools but it could not find a solution for many years.

member of Parliament: politician who is elected to sit in the House of Commons. During a general election, the country is divided up into ridings (or, constituencies). The voters in each riding elect one candidate to represent them in the government as their Member of Parliament.

Opposition: the party with the second most number of seats in the House of Commons. Its role is to provide a balance to the government in power. It maintains a shadow Cabinet that monitors the government and keeps it in check.

Paris Peace Conference, 1919: from January 18, 1919 to January 20, 1920, with a few breaks, members from the winning countries of World War I negotiated five peace treaties (one for each of the defeated powers) to end World War I.

Parliament of Canada: the governor general (as the Queen's representative), the Senate and the House of Commons together make up Canada's Parliament. Parliament makes laws that apply across the country.

Passchendaele, Battle of: a major battle of World War I, also known as the Third Battle of Ypres. It lasted from July 31 to November 10, 1917. The fight was for control of the village of Passchendaele in Belgium. After three months of fighting in marshy, muddy conditions with many lives lost on both sides, Canadian troops ended the battle when they took control of the village.

Perley, Sir George (1867–1938): Canadian politician and diplomat. He served as high commissioner to Great Britain and minister of the overseas military forces during Sir Robert Borden's term as prime minister.

Quebec nationalists: people who believe that the province of Quebec has a right to be a country independent of Canada.

reciprocity: or, free trade, an agreement between Canada and the United States that allows both countries to sell goods to the other country without being taxed by the other country. Without a reciprocity agreement, for example, if Canadian businessmen tried to sell blankets in the US, the American government might tax them and make them more expensive than American ones. Then, fewer people in the US would want to buy Canadian blankets.

Sifton, Sir Clifford (1861–1929): lawyer, politician, and newspaper owner. As Canada's minister of the interior between 1896 and 1905, Sifton persuaded the government to increase immigration in order to increase farm production in the West. To attract as many newcomers as possible, Sifton established Canadian offices throughout Britain, in some European countries and in the United States. He resigned in 1905 because he disagreed with his government's involvement in creating separate Catholic schools in the newly formed provinces of Alberta and Saskatchewan. He was knighted in 1915.

Smuts, Jan (1870–1950): prime minister of the Union of South Africa from 1919 to 1924 and from 1939 to 1948. He was responsible for the creation of the League of Nations and the later United Nations. He is the only person to sign both charters. He worked with Sir Robert Borden to create the British Commonwealth, which gave Britain's former colonies equal status with Great Britain.

For more information on the terms listed in this glossary, visit www.jackfruitpress.com

Still more words and facts you might want to know

Supreme Court of Nova Scotia: established in 1754, the highest court in Nova Scotia. It deals with cases that are usually larger or more serious than the lower courts deal with. It also hears appeals from the lower courts.

Thompson, Sir John Sparrow David (1845–94): Canada's fourth prime minister. Initially reluctant to enter politics, Thompson became prime minister in 1892 after the resignation of John Abbott. He died while on business in England.

Treaty of Versailles: the peace treaty that ended World War I. It was signed June 19, 1919 after six months of negotiations at the Paris Peace Conference. Fighting in the war stopped on November 11, 1918.

Tupper, Sir Charles (1821–1915): sixth prime minister of Canada for 69 days from May 1 to July 8, 1896. He was an early leader of the movement to unite British North American colonies and was one of the Fathers of Confederation.

Tupper, Sir Charles Hibbert (1855–1927): second son of Sir Charles Tupper, he became a Conservative MP and sat in the House of Commons for 22 years.

Unionist party: a party made up of Conservatives and pro-conscription Liberals. Created by Robert Borden in 1917, this party was formed for the purpose of passing conscription into law. An election was called in 1917, which the Unionist party won. Conscription was passed into law in 1917. The party's reason for existence ended when the war ended in 1918.

Western Front: a term used during World Wars I and II that meant where the boundary was between lands controlled by the Allies to the West and Germany to the East. For both world wars there was also an Eastern Front. The Western Front during most of World War I was from the English Channel to the Swiss border, through the west part of Belgium and down through France to Switzerland.

Women's Canadian Club of Montreal: a club that was started in 1907 to provide a place where women could learn about, discuss, and plan to act on political issues of Canada.

World War I (1914–1918): also known as the First World War, or the Great War. It was an international conflict that involved most of the countries of Europe as well as Russia, the United States, the Middle East, and other regions. The war pitted the Central Powers—mainly Germany, Austria-Hungary, and Turkey—against the Allies—mainly France, Great Britain (including Canada), Russia, Italy, Japan, and, from 1917, the United States. It ended with the defeat of the Central Powers.

Index: Where to find stuff in this book